HOME SERIES

HOME SERIES
MINIMAL LIVING

BETA-PLUS

CONTENTS

P. 4-5
A project by Nathalie Van Reeth. The open gas fireplace offers plenty of space above it for projecting films or photos.

P. 6
The entrance hall of Roos Blower's (Aerts + Blower) own house. The ground floor has polished concrete. A black wall divides this hall from the stairs, covered with MDF and finished with white Bolidt synthetics.

FOREWORD

inimalism emerged in the United States in the 1960s. The trend for minimalism began in the field of sculpture and soon became popular with painters.

The development was less quick to take hold within architecture, but it was no less significant: architects inspired by minimalism, such as John Pawson, Claudio Silvestrin, Peter Zumthor and Alberto Campo Baeza, brought about far-reaching changes in the world of contemporary architecture and interiors.

The power of simplicity is fundamental to minimalist living: the purest essence of the home and interior, with no redundancy or frills.

This book presents recently completed projects by leading architects and designers who have been influenced by minimalism: they are all worthy ambassadors of the "less is more" principle.

P. 8
This kitchen area annex breakfast corner is separated from the dining room by a half-height wall: separate and yet one. Realisation by interior decorator Christine Van Steen.

P. 10-11
Interior expert Ethel Van den Daele designed this penthouse apartment like a loft: transparent over the entire area, sober use of colours and materials. The apartment is only 40 m^2, but the structure of the penthouse leant itself to bare and open up the entire area.

LOFT INSPIRATION

T his metropolitan duplex apartment offers magnificent views and optimum incidence of light.

To create a feeling of intimacy, the larger rooms were divided into different areas while retaining the loft concept by not using fixed walls.

Although Nathalie Van Reeth selected different materials, she used the same tonality to preserve the loft's atmosphere so that the different areas blend together; a whole picture that radiates peace and serenity.

The spectacular staircase is one of Nathalie Van Reeth's creations.

Salon and TV-area are separated by an open cupboard set that simultaneously creates intimacy. All furniture, the fireplace and stairs were created by Nathalie Van Reeth.

P. 14-15
Behind the sliding wall with fireplace there is a
space for a TV and sound system.
Vintage furniture and a vintage Iranian carpet.

A sitting corner with PK22 white leather chairs by
Poul Kjaerholm and a vintage table.

The low table was created by
Ado Chale in cooperation with
Nathalie Van Reeth: inspired by
the search for new materials.

The vintage reclining chair was designed by Mies van der Rohe. On the left a vintage table and a lamp by Christian Liaigre. The piece of art is by Jean-Marc Bustamante.

P. 20-21
View of the dining room.

A playful mix of white and black for the library/office.

Reading corner with white linen chaise longue on a vintage carpet.

The open kitchen, designed by Nathalie Van Reeth, can be closed off from the dining area thanks to a large sliding door. Wall units in tinted glass, island and kitchen counter in polished inox. Bar stools Lem and a Boffi cooking unit.

P. 24-25
The open shower with adjacent
hammam is designed fully in small
black marble mosaic.

The ultimate feeling of the luxury of a hotel room.

The children's room and the bathrooms each have their own colour accents, yet the same materials were selected: glass mosaic and stained Carrara marble. Vola faucets and wall light by Cubetto.

A SOBER, TIMELESS ATMOSPHERE

A In an apartment building on an old factory site Dries Dols realised a sober, timeless interior in which the industrial epoxy floor contrasts with the warm, solid wood.

A kitchen design in one line, constructed from identical, white lacquered panels which conceal handle-free drawers and cupboards. A work surface made from white composite stone.

The kitchen annex dining area with a table and walls from solid oak, an epoxy floor and a kitchen lined with composite stone. Light fittings from Lightyears and cushions from Smarin Livingstones. Stools from Quinze & Milan Special.

White curtains from Treveria, a carpet from Bic Carpets, furniture from Tacchini, Moroso, Vitra (model Cité designed by Jean Prouvé) and Modular lighting.

On the background to the left a solid oak door wall. The table is also made from solid oak planks. An epoxy floor, hanging lamps from Lightyears in Denmark and on the far left a few cushions from Smarin Livingstones. The dining room chairs are the famous Eames classics, Plastic Side Chair, from 1961.

A "box bath" with shower wall treated to protect against moisture. Solid oak doors with milled handles. Epoxy floor, cabinets and other custom-made objects in Colorcore.

The handles on these solid oak doors were milled. Epoxy floor and black MDF worktop. White Treveria curtains. Dynamobel Dis chairs and rubber desktops.

LIGHT, COLOURFUL AND TRENDY

R oos Blower (Aerts + Blower) transformed a maisonette from 1963 into a light and trendy house, with a wink back to the 1960's.

The dining room floor continues on the terrace: when the doors are open, inside becomes outside. The chairs and wall size photograph of a hamburger restaurant on Route 66 refer to the sixties. The steel spiral staircase connects this area to the living room above, where the orange glass balustrade on the landing provides an additional touch of colour.

The kitchen was designed completely by Aerts + Blower and finished by Wille-interieur.
The furniture is made from high gloss Formica laminate. The green cooking niche contrasts with the white cupboards and provides a colour accent.

The bathroom walls were covered in five layers of paint by Boss Paints; they glitter in the daylight entering via the skylight above the shower. A rain shower and the toilet are behind the blue glass.

The orange in the built-in wardrobe and seat create a lively living room. The floor has been seamlessly moulded across the entire storey. All light sources have been incorporated indirectly into the ceiling.

The bedroom is in its simplicity sober and chic at the same time.

The desk borders the living area and offers a nice garden view.

A THOROUGH METAMORPHOSIS

 A classical residence underwent a thorough metamorphosis, spurred on by Nathalie Van Reeth.

The house was fully stripped, down to the basic structure.

The rear was torn open to strengthen the contact with the sunny garden and improve the incidence of light. Materials and colour were added subtly to accentuate the serene atmosphere.

A modest atmosphere in the entrance hall. Whitewashed walls, dark aged oak boards on the floor and black/white photos.

The dining area with a tinted oak table, chairs by Marie's Corner and a black leather carpet by Limited Edition.

Salon and dining room gently flow over into each other, the linear table and the fireplace connect both areas. Two black leather PK22 seats by Poul Kjaerholm.

The salon looks out over a water feature. Seats and tables according to designs by Nathalie Van Reeth. The chauffeuses are by Christian Liaigre. An antique Afghan carpet and a vintage chair.

P. 52-53
The kitchen harmoniously mixes
traditional and modern elements.

A bathroom in Calacatta marble designed by Nathalie Van Reeth. MEM faucets by Dornbracht and lighting by Cubetto.

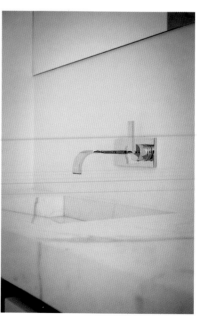

The dressing was custom made according to a design by Nathalie Van Reeth. Cupboards in high-shine varnish with a tinted oak veneer finish for the interior.

Children's rooms with custom made furniture in varnished MDF, yet with Missoni accents for girls and Libeco grey linen for boys.

Fresh colours in this bathroom with wood painted white and bright azure blue glass mosaic.

A MINIMALIST PERSPECTIVE

I n this report, three different minimalist interiors designed by Minus are presented.

In this rural home, designed by Minus, an open plan has been chosen, to optimize the access to the spaces, as well as to maximize the contact between the inside and outside. From the open pivoting door, you have a view from the entrace into the living space. The mounted Kreon light fittings emphasise the perspective.

This project, in the historical centre of Ghent, was designed to fit the occupants, with respect to their collection of art and design furniture.

The private home of the interior architects Sophie Popelier and Wim Carton fits in with the offices and the production of Minus. The house translates into practice the vision of living and working, the lines and materials. The table was tailor made in laminate, together with chairs, by B&B Italy. The narrow entrance provides a sluice between living and working.

The feeling of space in this realisation of Minus is also intensified by the open kitchen and the finish of the living space which runs through into the kitchen section. The cooking zone also has a breakfast corner.

The kitchen in Sophie Popelier and Wim Carton's own home. The illumination strip behind the steam section allows the sunlight to enter and shine on the washing and cooking zone. The kitchen concept includes a cooking section and a closed wall with sliding doors. The kitchen connects the dining and living space. The Inox sink is tailor-made and equipped with a lower section for the Vola taps.

The floor and the kitchen worktop are designed in white marble and the cupboards in dark wood veneers, to contrast with the white sliding doors. Each sliding door, when opened, provides a unit with another function. A Minus project.

Diagonal to the entrance is the entry to the dining area thanks to the glass panels. Chairs from Vitra. The dining room is perpendicular to the kitchen. The open stair construction emphasises the void on the first floor.

P. 70-71
Next to the sink section, the breakfast table with garden view.

This bathroom, designed by
Minus, plays with volumes and
glass walls. The bath is also
completely tailor-made.

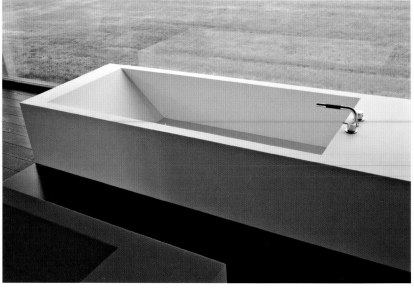

Another bathroom project by Minus.

The offices of Minus' design studio.
The enclosed space of the studio with reception areas is completely designed in LG. The inside of the cupboards is in dark laminate. Above: the reception desk with a dark wood veneer section and grey glass. The walls are provided with illumination strips. They have a deep-set plinth in the colour of the dark cast floor. The large windows and glass walls give the offices great transparency and openness to nature.

This notary's practice was designed by Minus with strict lines and executed in warm materials and colours to give a homely and inviting atmosphere.
In the entrance hall the veneer wall runs from the sofa to the reception desk.
In all areas, the contrast between the light and dark material was the guide.

AN OASIS OF PEACE AND SERENITY

An existing, classical residence in the Antwerp area was thoroughly renovated by Nathalie Van Reeth.

All areas flow over into each other and form one whole by using different materials that have been treated to obtain the same colour tonality: from grey to greige, from black to white.

The result is an oasis of peace and serenity.

A large desk designed in dark stained oak under the windows on the street side. A library cupboard by Ethnicraft was painted black. Chairs by Christian Liaigre around a table of volcanic stone.

Salon and dining area form an open whole; the aged boarded floor runs through without carpets to prevent interrupting the continuity. Two grey brown seats by Christian Liaigre and a canapé designed by Nathalie Van Reeth.

The multifunctional (sleeping / working / playing) attic studio was painted completely white to create a strong sense of space.

The dressing room in black/white-shades.

The entrance hall with a custom made cloak cupboard and a washbasin, both designed by Nathalie Van Reeth and constructed out of different materials manipulated in such a way that they still obtained the same tonality.

The floating top serves as a desk and bookrack.

Both children's rooms were designed by Nathalie Van Reeth, with furniture in stained oak.

Bathroom in lye-treated wood and a piece of washbasin furniture in blue ashler designed by Nathalie Van Reeth. Vola faucet.

A bathroom with hammam-shower in black zelliges and with a washbasin in black slate. MEM faucet by Dornbracht.

SURPRISINGLY SPACIOUS

Bart Van Boom (Kultuz) realised the complete metamorphosis of an existing home. The entire living area, from cellar to attic, was revised and suddenly became "surprisingly spacious".

The minimalist finish exudes calm, the perspectives have been optimised. The artwork by Maurice Frydman in the living room is the eye catcher. The open fireplace has been integrated in the wall together with a multimedia furniture, architecturally set in the existing walls.

P. 94-95
The existing radiators were boxed in and painted in the colour of the walls.

A modest counter element was added to this kitchen, designed by Kultuz: the children can do their homework here but guests can also sit here so that the host and hostess can continue to work in the kitchen undisturbed and still keep contact.

The combination of wood veneer with white lacquer and a natural stone surface fits with the choice of colour and material in the living area, which makes the open kitchen increase the comfort of living even further.

Tranquillity and serenity in this bathroom design by Kultuz, with equivalent comfort for both the master and the children's bathrooms, but with personal touches for both rooms.

LUXURY AND REFINEMENT

Interior architect Isabelle Onraet argues for sober, timeless designs, that also exude luxury, refinement and harmony in a homely, convivial atmosphere.

For this client, a passionate flower arranger, Isabelle Onraet created a neutral colour scheme that makes it possible to change the decoration often.

P. 100-103
The oak hearth wall was stained dark, with sliding doors on the left and right in the same colour as the wall. The parquet floor was oiled white. Chairs and coffee table from Maxalto on a linen carpet. The small chairs, the side tables and the lights are by Christian Liaigre.

A table in dark stained oak and chairs by Promemoria (at 'Aksent). The parquet flooring was oiled white.

A breakfast corner with table and chairs by Promemoria (at 'Aksent), wooden panelling with built-in fridge and a desk surface in the furthest corner. A realisation by Isabelle Onraet, all custom-made by Devaere.

A dining table in dark oak and chairs are by Maxalto. The artwork is by G. Leclef.

Two kitchen designs by Isabelle Onraet.
Left page: cupboard fronts in an oak finish (dark stain) with 8 cm thick work surfaces in bluestone (lightened finish). A varnished parquet floor and bluestone tiles in the kitchen area, also lightened. The extractor fan was integrated in a frame, which makes the filters invisible. Finish: Interieur Maddens.
Right page: this kitchens was finished by Devaere in sandblasted and pale tinted larch. Both the floor and the kitchen work surface are made from the ssame dark brown natural stone. The American fridge was integrated completely in the larch, with the wine fridges, the combi-oven and steamer beside it.

Guest and master bathroom in a penthouse, designed by interior architect Isabelle Onraet.
In the guest bathroom, white varnish and similar paintwork is combined with light-lilac mosaic. The washbasins and shower in the master bathroom were coated in white Silestone Blanco Zeus.
The bedroom shows wengé cubes as floor covering with bed and bedside cabinets in the master bedroom in dark tinted oak, customised by Devaere.

A MONOCHROME SEASIDE VILLA

A picturesque villa on the Belgian coast was thoroughly restored.

The outer volume and the appearance of the residence had to remain identical so as to not disturb the existing coast style and the image of the village.

The clients asked Nathalie Van Reeth to design a true family home, to which many friends are invited and where there is enough space to organise a party and stay for the night.

The volumes were reconsidered, the attic was utilised and the basements were dug out to create extra storage space.

The limited number of materials and the monochrome colour pallet create a sober, taut whole.

A sober image with modest colours and natural materials. Seats by Flexform and tables by Interni around a fireplace, finished in rough concrete. The curtains and seat material were designed in coarse linen.

The open kitchen, with a central island that serves as a bar and an extra piece of storage furniture, is also one of Nathalie Van Reeth's creations. A fireplace for a barbecue, finished on the inside with rough concrete. The fridge is fully integrated in the wall system: a taut whole. Work tablets and kitchen floor in a brown, solid sandstone. Chocolate brown curtains in coarse linen. Bar stools and chairs by Marie's Corner.

The bedroom with open dressing area. The cupboards with pivoting doors are designed in varnished MDF and finished on the inside with aged oak. The oak wooden floor is also aged. Blinds in linen.

The children's rooms are located in the attic space. The roof framing is finished in roughly planed, white painted boards. Boarded floor in aged oak. Furniture in varnished MDF.

The attic floor is the children's exclusive territory; an open play and reception area, with an XXL-sofa that also serves as a futon for friends, with another fold out bed under it.

All bathrooms radiate the same sober monastic atmosphere. All floors, washbasins and bathtubs have a brown sandstone finish. The walls have been cemented evenly.

AN IDEAL BLEND

RR Interieur is a furniture shop specialised in contemporary furniture from top brands. RR also realises customised projects with an ideal blend of timelessness, durability, refinement and comfort. This report shows three different projects by this leading Belgian design agency.

RR Interieur chose a solid table designed by Bart Lens with Pausa chairs by Flexform in this villa in Knokke-Zoute, in partnership with interior architect Nathalie Deboel. RR works exclusively with Kevin Reilly lighting. In the background, garden furniture from Piet Boon.

The large lights above the dining table are a creation by Bart Lens. Hanging sideboard in high gloss lacquer from Poliform. All the furniture was selected by RR Interieur.

A white Flexform sofa (Groundpiece model) and on the right a Lifesteel lounge suite, also from Flexform. The wrought iron window separates the open plan kitchen from the living rooms. An RR project in collaboration with interior architect Nathalie Deboel.

A canapé Magnum from Flexform in this loft on the sea embankment of Knokke-Zoute.

The B&O flat screen and the open fireplace from De Puydt were integrated harmoniously in the solid made to measure furniture and panelling.

P. 120-121
Two armchairs from Flexform (Mozart model) and the Groundpiece sofa, also from Flexform. The solid coffee tables and console table were tailor made by RR. A design hearth from De Puydt. Lighting from Foscarini, candelabre B&B Objects, vases from Flexform.

A chair by Flexform (model Emily).

An open kitchen, custom-made in solid
wood, with a solid custom-made table from
RR Interieur and chairs from Hans Wegner.
A project in partnership with interior
architect Nathalie Deboel.

HOME SERIES

Volume 17 : MINIMAL LIVING

The reports in this book are selected from the Beta-Plus collection of home-design books: www.betaplus.com
They have been compiled in a special series by Le Figaro in French language: Ma Déco

Copyright © 2009 Beta-Plus Publishing / Le Figaro
Originally published in French language

PUBLISHER
Beta-Plus Publishing
Termuninck 3
B – 7850 Enghien
Belgium
www.betaplus.com
info@betaplus.com

TEXT
Alexandra Druesne

PHOTOGRAPHY
Jo Pauwels

DESIGN
Polydem - Nathalie Binart

TRANSLATIONS
Txt-Ibis

ISBN: 978-90-8944-048-8

Printed in China

P. 126-127
A Boffi-kitchen in an interior created by Collection Privée.